MW00776808

My Name is Karl

Susan Giesecke

BookLocker
St. Petersburg, Florida

Copyright © 2020 Susan Giesecke

Print ISBN: 978-1-64719-116-0
Epub ISBN: 978-1-64719-117-7
Mobi ISBN: 978-1-64719-118-4

All rights reserved. No part of this publication may be reproduced, stored in a retrieval system, or transmitted in any form or by any means, electronic, mechanical, recording or otherwise, without the prior written permission of the author.

Published by BookLocker.com, Inc., St. Petersburg, Florida.
Book cover designed by Bede Van Dyke

Printed on acid-free paper.

BookLocker.com, Inc.
2020

First Edition

Library of Congress Cataloguing in Publication Data
Giesecke, Susan
My Name is Karl by Susan Giesecke
Library of Congress Control Number: 2020921331

Table of Contents

Introduction

What does it mean to be human? In our age of technology and gene splicing, philosophers and geneticists alike ponder the uniqueness of each human being.

The gift of a child is an extraordinary event. Often taken for granted, only in retrospect can we appreciate how the combination and interaction of genetics, environment, and events create an individual. I often say the challenge of raising a child is humbling because you don't know for thirty years if you are doing it right. And sometimes there is no right.

Two questions come to mind as I share this very personal story. Why? And why now?

For the past fifteen years there has been a tugging in my heart to share Karl's story. Not so much his story, as the story of those who loved him and were in turn loved by him. I felt our family was stronger and more compassionate because of him.

There is a peace that comes from answering the tugging of the heart; a resolution and completion. On the flip side, there is that hope that a reader here and there will smile or say, "I understand."

And there is a maturity in letting the story out, allowing it to stretch wings and fly.

As President Joe Biden said in July 2016, "Trust me, there will come a day when you think of your loved family member, a smile will cross your face before the tear runs down your cheek."

Sunday Morning, February 21, 2010

Sunday was Karl's favorite day because it meant church, hand bells, ushering and "holding" the door as congregational members went in and out of the Fellowship Hall following worship service.

Karl was the "mascot" of Holy Cross, deemed so by Gene Fogt, his personal friend and long-standing pastor. Everybody knew and loved Karl. He had been baptized and confirmed at Holy Cross. He'd challenged the Sunday School teachers, volunteered at Vacation Bible School and worked in the Food Pantry.

Karl lived with us, his parents, on the second story of our home. We wanted him to maintain his independence, but still be available for meals, maintain a schedule, and have family support.

So, when he came down the stairs on that Sunday morning complaining he had a headache, I knew it was true. Every other Sunday, he was the first up reminding the rest of the family it was Sunday!

This was not the first headache Karl had had. About six times a year he experienced headaches, so we had developed a routine: a bed was made on the couch so we could be close and we began a regimen of medication.

All day he rested, drinking an Ensure Plus or two, but not showing any signs of getting better. Even this was not unusual because sometimes it would take two to three days for him to come around.

The operative word was *patience*.

Windy

Who's peekin' out from under a stairway
Calling a name that's lighter than air
Who's bending down to give me a rainbow
Everyone knows it's Windy.

Who's tripping down the streets of the city
Smilin' at everybody he sees
Who's reaching out to capture a moment?
Everyone knows it's Windy

And Windy has stor-my eyes
That flash at the sound of lies
And Windy has wings to fly
Above the clouds, Above the clouds.

—The Association

Karl at age 10 *Picture taken by his brother Kevin*

At 1:00 a.m. on Tuesday, September 11, 1968, my husband Noel and I were sitting in the hospital parking lot, trying to figure out if the strange pains I was having were, in fact, labor pains. After delivering two children, this was a bit of a surprise, to be wondering. The popular song, *Windy*, was playing on the radio.

The physician kept saying, "It's too early. This baby's too small." By Tuesday afternoon, we were on our way home again. Even the birth of this child gave the word *patience* new meaning.

But Friday evening, the pains were real, and Karl was born at 3:10 in the morning, weighing 4 pounds and 8 ounces. His birth followed a difficult pregnancy complete with medication "to help the baby," my total exhaustion, easily explained by Karl's older siblings, a four year old sister Laura, and an active three year old brother Kevin, along with the uneasy feeling that something just didn't feel quite right. His father recalls Karl's little body jerking fitfully and also remarked, "I could hold him in the palm of my hand."

His name was to be Karl Lee Giesecke. Where did we get that name? We had friends named Carl and Lee, but the main influence was a German friend, Willu, whose father was named Karl. She is bright, charming, beautiful and willing to stand up for her beliefs. We admired her. Her father Karl was handsome in a Germanic way. And with the surname Giesecke, Karl with a K seemed to fit.

Karl was welcomed into our very traditional middle-class family of German descent. Noel, his father, was a fledging dentist in Houston and his Mom, me, a teacher. Karl's sister Laura was riding a bicycle at 4½ and his brother Kevin was born taking charge. We lived in a neighborhood full of young families with multiple children.

When I looked into his infant eyes, I thought, "this is an old soul." Then, I had no idea what that might mean or why I had that feeling. Even today, as I write these words, I cannot explain it.

Little did we know then the impact this wee one would have on our lives and the lives of the many people who came to love him.

Because he was low weight and suffered some jaundice, he remained in the preemie ward for two weeks. When we went to the hospital to bring him home, I commented, "it looks and feels like we're adopting a child." This *adoption* introduced a whole world of *adapting* into our lives!

His first year was challenging with many colds and infections, and his development was slow. However, by 16 months, he walked and at 18 months said his first word, "boat."

And yet, by the time Karl was fourteen months old, I realized his development was too slow. Following a consultation with the pediatrician, we were admitted to Texas Children's Hospital for tests. Texas Children's is the hospital of last resort for children suffering from unusual and/or abnormal symptoms. The physicians were superb, with a special expertise in children's issues. Many patients and their families had spent weeks and months there. It was a community. Over three days there, we received quite an education. Parents shared and bonded in an amazing fashion. The situations faced by these families seemed to have been taken straight from a medical textbook. My mind couldn't get around their stories. "My child's situation is terminal," "There is no medication for his condition," "We have been here a year now." How do people deal with this?

By the end of three days, I can still remember the blunt, matter-of-fact manner of the physician who announced, "He's mentally retarded." I was devastated. Our pediatrician had been saying Karl was all right and his overly anxious Mom must learn to "calm down."

As I tried to recall what mental retardation meant, I had little frame of reference. As an elementary school child, I recalled the Talent Preservation Class in our school, populated by children who were separated from the rest of us. One boy seemed to hug the wall as he walked down the hall and was surprised when I said "Hi" to him. He looked normal to me.

Then there was Garth Davis in high school. His Mom was the math teacher everybody loved, so he was tolerated because of her. And, when I taught sixth grade, a special student, Joe Lee Bailey, was an integral part of one class. His parents did not want him separated from his peers or placed in a special class. Prior teachers had prepared the students so well that Joe Lee was truly accepted. One day he recited accurately all the states and their respective capitals. His joy was real, and our cheers made his achievement complete. We all loved Joe Lee. And he returned the love.

Meanwhile a pastor who came to visit said prophetically, "We all have disabilities in some area … Everyone isn't a master at everything."

Tuesday, February 23, 2010

"We've got to go…"

The Monday following the 21st of February 2010, was a repeat of Sunday. The headache was still severe.

Some liquid, no response. Karl had slept most of the day. Noel began the next routine, an antibiotic. In the past, the antibiotic had always seemed to help, even though it frequently took a couple of days.

Because of his dental connections, we were able to keep antibiotics on hand for these emergencies. Over the years, we lost track of the times Karl would become lethargic and listless. The many times his eyes would roll back in his head. He endured hospital stays with sophisticated tests and exams without definitive results. What a brave young fellow!

By Tuesday, February 23rd, I said, "Noel, it's time to go to the hospital…"

By the time we were admitted, his blood pressure was very low, and he was put on IV's immediately for dehydration.

Karl's Firsts...

As a teacher in a self-contained classroom, I was keenly aware of learning differences. Children learn differently because they are different. Now, in my own family, we are experiencing *differentness*. Laura and Kevin, Karl's older siblings developed normally.

I also learned that bright students learned whether I was there to teach or not. The slower students, however, learned because of the teacher. This was quite an insight for me prompting me to become acutely aware of the importance of knowing the student so well you knew how to present the material in a way he/she could hear and understand.

So, when Karl learned a new skill for the first time, we were ecstatic. The thrill of achievement in his eyes and on his face made all the effort worthwhile.

Karl progressed, ever so slowly, and we celebrated!

Speech was also a slow process. Karl said "Mama" in July of 1970, when he was almost two. In October 1970, testing determined he had mild to moderate hearing loss. After a tonsillectomy and PE tubes were inserted to allow drainage from the inner ear, Karl "heard" much better. When he came home from the hospital following the surgery, he physically jumped into my arms when he heard the grandfather clock chime for the first time.

In May 1975, Karl spoke two sentences, a five-word total!

And, in September 1975, our fourth child, Michael Allen, was born. His arrival prompted another *evaluation*—this time the chromosomes. Karl's were normal as were Michael's. A new medical procedure, amino synthesis was also performed, letting us know that Michael was as normal as they come. Everyone in the family enjoyed watching Michael do all the things babies do... on time!

Karl moved to an Educatable Mentally Retarded (EMR) class in Spring Branch. He learned a new phrase from this brother Kevin, "you stink!" It was funny and appropriate because so often Karl did stink.

The teenage years for Karl were very difficult, in part because he was mainstreamed into a *normal* Physical Education class. This brought out a violent streak where Karl would grab a knife, pull his arm back in a very threatening gesture. I was slow to connect the two events. Finally, I consulted with the school staff and had him removed from the PE class. The threatening behavior stopped immediately.

Several years later, Karl's fascination with firearms prompted him to patrol the neighborhood, with a toy pistol. A pair of binoculars and a list of license plate numbers kept him occupied. In fact, some of the neighbors expressed pleasure that he kept track of happenings on the block. However, one evening at 8:30, a city policeman named Mike showed up at our door. Apparently, Karl had held a very realistic looking toy pistol to two workmen across the street on April 4, 2002. He was "patrolling" and did not recognize them as neighbors and thought they might be causing trouble. The workmen were frightened. How sobering! How tragic this could have been.

What if the workmen had had real guns, as so many folks do? Fortunately, the policeman, Mike, had a developmentally challenged child himself, and understood. In addition, our neighbors had spoken kindly of Karl, so no charges were filed. Mike left the police dispatcher's phone number so Karl could call if he saw anything suspicious in the neighborhood.

We became acutely aware of the risks faced by "challenged" people in our society, since much of Karl's life was spent in an imaginary world, populated with Superheroes, movie stars, and fantasy people. He often could not separate the real world from his imaginary world.

A few weeks later, in the interest of transparency, I decided to tell our other children about the experience with the toy pistol. By then, 2002, we had become a family of adults. The older children were married, and Laura was already the mother of a 2-year-old daughter, Madison. Their responses were genuine. How do we help Karl understand? How do we protect him? How does he separate his internal imaginary world from the real external world?

At age 35, Karl was still experiencing "firsts." A deteriorating hearing loss prompted an evaluation that resulted in his getting a hearing aid. He tried it for a while, and the aid appeared to be helping him to hear. Then he abruptly refused to wear it. When I asked why, his response was that those were for old people. Then I began to listen to the small talk conversation Karl was missing. I suspect he figured out he wasn't missing a lot of important information. And, if it was important, I'd touch him, look him in the eyes and talk into his good ear.

He enjoyed his private world of music and imaginary friends.

Karl at age 3

Changes...

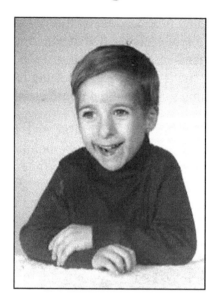

Karl at age 5

There was a quality of "Windy-ness" to living with Karl, an unpredictability that required a great deal of patience from his entire circle of family and friends. Everyone was alert and acutely aware of where Karl was and what he might be doing. Then, as time went on, it became apparent that Karl played a big part in the development of his "family."

The family Karl helped develop was composed of his father, Noel, a tall good-looking Texan who was quiet and not prone to show emotion. One exception, however, was his high level of perfectionism, perfect for dentistry but a difficult challenge in daily life. Between the intricacies of a dental practice and the foibles of family life, Noel would often become angry, mostly at himself, he said, as he tried to make everything perfect. His mother was also a perfectionist, so he chose a wife who wasn't.

And I'm sure that produced its own set of challenges for him because I could tolerate chaos if that was the choice between visiting with a friend or cleaning house. Even before Karl was born, it was clear that I was not in the same league with Noel's mother when it came to keeping the house clean.

Laura was born in 1964, beautiful and physically totally normal. She walked at ten and a half months and was a joy. Kevin, born thirteen and a half months later, was blond and totally boy. He loved cars and trains and shared his father's perfectionism. Laura and Kevin were four and three respectively when Karl was born in 1968. Michael, born seven years later was an unexpected gift to our family. He was a joy because he was so normal. If the average age for a baby to get a first tooth was six months, Michael's first tooth came in at six months. He was a textbook case. We four would surround him, just to watch him roll over or crawl.

So, the relationship between Karl and the other family members was very interesting, to say the least. How did Karl get along with his siblings? What about their *peers?* One anecdote went like this:

"Mom, why wasn't Karl in the Sunday School Christmas program this year?"

"Well, Kevin, remember last year when Karl was singing and playing his imaginary guitar, and everyone laughed at him?"

"Yes, all the kids in my class laughed."

"At Karl?"

"No, at me, because Karl is my brother."

"I don't think you need to go through that again either."

And another: Laura went to Bible Camp and seemed to thoroughly enjoy the experience. One boy, brain damaged, was there. The other campers made fun of him, and he went home on Wednesday. Laura was very observant. "Mama, never send Karl to Bible Camp."

Since Michael was seven years younger than Karl, they experienced a unique relationship. Karl loved to walk Michael to school, and Michael's development challenged Karl to try new activities and skills. This special relationship became very apparent when Michael was planning his wedding for May 2008. He asked both his brothers to stand with him as groomsmen. When his bride chose her sister as her one attendant, Michael wondered how to handle the situation. I suggested perhaps Karl would be happy as the usher since he had experience as an usher at church worship services. As the situation was presented to Karl, his response was quick and decisive. "I'm Michael's Best Man and Kevin is the Assistant Best Man. And so, it was. And the best MEN were outstanding.

"Best Men"

As our grandchildren came along, Uncle Karl became a favorite. He had great toys and loved to play dolls. The first three grandchildren were girls. When the third granddaughter was announced, Karl was relieved. He knows *girls*. And they loved him. "Kawl" was Emily's first word, and Madison would often ask, "What about Karl?" whenever an activity was planned.

Has Karl affected the lives of our family who have nurtured and loved him? The answer is a resounding, "yes!" Our responses, however, are as varied as we are. Noel, Karl's Dad, feels a strong sense of responsibility for Karl's life, even over his own. In addition, he reports that he now recognizes that unexpected events occur in everyone's lives. No one is unscathed or survives alone.

Laura, Karl's only sister, chose a career as a teacher in Special Education. Statistics indicate that 80% of the oldest daughters in families with handicapped members choose a career in the helping fields—teaching, social work and nursing. She brought to her work an empathy few can match. In fact, her sibling relationship was a concern when she applied for a teaching position. Some in the school district felt she might be too empathic. But, coupled with that empathy was firmness and respect for her students. Laura recognized the importance of encouraging task responsibility and pushing each student to be his or her best. She also recognized in herself a growing anger toward educational systems that lack understanding and a society that needs to be more enlightened.

Kevin acknowledges that he is able to be more accepting and understanding of differences in people. Not only is Kevin a man with a great sense of humor, he rarely says anything negative and is not critical of other people. He seems willing to look at behavior and its causes rather than to being judgmental. He is quick to offer help and assistance to those in need.

Michael has had, perhaps, the most difficult task as a sibling. As Karl's younger brother, his concerns as a child were unique. Once he shared his fear that he would wake up one morning and be like Karl. When asked if having Karl as a brother made a difference in his life, he responded. "Well, people laugh at him and make fun of him. Then, when people see me with him, they start talking and making fun of me because I'm his brother."

These amazing children have become very caring compassionate adults. They have married wonderful spouses who share their values; people who accepted and loved Karl as their own brother. I often felt our children were mature beyond their years because of Karl; because they learned to be considerate and compensate toward others. They also seemed to understand life. To their credit, they accepted their brother and his "specialness."

As Karl's mother, I know my life is much different than it would have been. The extra time and effort spent raising him has taught me that everyone has a profound effect on those around them. The patience and persistence required, however, humbly offered and practiced, taught me that mentally challenged people do learn, although more slowly, and respond with a wholesome celebration in their achievements. Above all, I learned about love—that forgiving, self-sacrificing, glory-in-the-progress-of-others kind of love that actually forms the foundation of family and society the world over.

Yes, there was a "Windy" quality to our life with Karl. And he did redefine *patience* for all of us. And, too, there was joy. His father recounted, "I can still 'fix' things for Karl. "Tis a gift to be simply needed."

The Family: Karl, Michael, Kevin and Laura.

Front row: Susan and Noel

Wednesday, February 24th, 2010

Visitation hours in the ICU were strictly limited to three twenty-minute opportunities each day. Spring Branch Hospital was in our neighborhood, an institution of the community for 50 years. While some people complained that the hospital wasn't 21st century, many others in the community knew and loved this facility. It was like the comfortable family physician who would make house calls in an emergency. Neighbors worked there and people knew you by name.

Once the staff realized Karl was not able to communicate his needs, we were allowed to stay with him 24/7.

What a gift, because Wednesday at noon, he quit breathing.

Noel and I were sitting at the foot of his bed, and I noticed it first. "Noel, he's not breathing." After I noticed it three times, I went to the nurses. "He's not breathing!"

Just like *ER* on television, all the bells and whistles shouted, "Code Blue!" Within minutes, teams of people attended him. We were sent to the waiting room to make way for the professionals.

Sitting in the outer room, terrified and stunned, we awaited news, and when Laura arrived, there was comfort in the fact that we were together. Thirty minutes later, a technician came to tell us Karl was now on a respirator, a breathing machine, to keep him alive.

21

Do What Works—Whatever it takes...

Blessed are the flexible,
For they shall never be bent out of shape.

Noel and I both come from strong, authoritarian German families who believed in discipline and obedience. In addition, our two older children, Laura and Kevin, had responded well to that structure. What a surprise when Karl not only failed to respond to discipline, but even seemed to deliberately provoke confrontation. He was unable to recognize a relationship between cause and effect or understand why anyone might be angry with him. On the other hand, we could not imagine how he could disobey again and again—after we were convinced he *knew better* and had even been punished.

Being college-educated professionals, we sought guidance from books. Even though some books were helpful in defining the problem and sharing one author's point of view, we ultimately learned that "each situation is unique, and no solution is *cast in stone.*" We must look upon our situation as a process; not a problem.

With Karl, traditional rules and discipline did not work. The classic adage "spare the rod and spoil the child" proved to be a failure and contributed to many traumatic family scenes.

Finally, one psychologist helped us to see that our goal was to enable Karl to develop as a person. We must be prepared to do whatever it takes to accomplish that goal as a family and as parents. It was good advice for all parents and people, we thought.

As a result, instead of shouting, "Don't touch that vase!" we moved the vase. Instead of demanding that all the toys be picked up, we removed all the toys, allowing only one or two at a time. Instead of a large gathering of people, which usually prompted serious hyperactivity and acting-out, we limited our entertaining to a short timeframe, or to a small group of people, or an after-bedtime event. Rather than expecting Karl to learn by observation or by our simple directives, we began to teach him in short sessions; breaking a task into steps and using constant repetition to *set* each behavior pattern. Karl worked on table setting for six months—one small task at a time. For years, he was in charge of setting the table and did it perfectly every time.

"Doing what worked" also involved great cooperation among the family, because Karl required consistency and constant prompting and encouragement for his personal growth. The goal was his attainment of independence and self-sufficiency. In spite of our discouragement at times, we learned that once our commitment to a goal had been made, the path to reaching that goal became clearer. However, whether we reached it or not depended on our level of commitment and our perseverance. Interestingly enough, this approach of setting priorities and realistic goals continues to help each of us accomplish difficult tasks in other areas of our lives as well.

Special times were vacations and holidays because they brought new experiences and unexpected events. Because of Karl's disabilities, structure was a very important value when it came to helping him cope with daily life. As a corollary, it became very important to prepare him carefully for any changes in the schedule. And there were many changes.

Most vacations revolved around the cabin and the lake house. The cabin, a gift from Noel's family, was in Colorado, very remote and very rustic. Karl would sleep upstairs in the bunk room, with sometimes as many as ten other people. It was a wonderful retreat center and a gathering place for family and friends. When we were there, everyone had to be flexible to get along. It was at the cabin that we learned that Karl had a very good eye and could shoot targets quite accurately. He also learned to ride a dirt bike.

At the cabin, Karl's father and the other deer hunters accepted Karl as one of the boys. This acceptance was perhaps one of the key turning points of his life. Until then, unrealistic expectations had ruled the day. "When would Karl snap out of it?" "Why can't he…?" The new reality meant that Karl was at last accepted for who he was, not what we wanted him to be. It was a giant step forward for us. While this change may have been subtle, the effect was tremendous. Today, studies show how important a father's role is in determining a child's well-being, and Karl's improvement was proof-positive!

One brief story illustrates how the extended family adapted to include Karl in every activity: Mountain climbing became a focal point for Michael and Brett, Laura's husband. The cabin was located in Chaffee County, Colorado, home of more "14ers" than any other Colorado County. "14 ers" means mountains that are over 14,000 feet tall. Each year these two "boys" would climb a mountain or two, which could prove to be quite a challenge. Routes can be difficult to follow, the atmosphere is relatively thin, and the hikers had to be in excellent physical condition. The climbers would leave the cabin at 5:00 am or so because the climb had to be completed before the afternoon rains moved into the mountains.

Brett and Michael would return exhausted and take a well-deserved nap. By evening we would be celebrating their achievement. Karl was the official awarder of a pin specific to the mountain climbed, and he would preface his presentation with some jokes he'd read or a comment or two. Michael and Brett were the perfect recipients, sunburned, rugged and appreciative.

The other family retreat is the Lakehouse, located on Lake LBJ, formerly Granite Shoals in central Texas. My grandfather bought the original lot, and my parents and brother built the original house in 1963 from the first story of a two-story San Antonio home facing demolition. Later a channel was dug to provide water access to the main body of the lake from the house.

This was where Karl overcame his fear of the water, learned to play billiards with me, and participated in shows presented by the children for the adults. Karl's contribution would be playing a selection on the Yamaha portable keyboard. Every holiday a different combination of friends and relatives celebrated, and Karl was an integral part of the festivities.

Christmas presented Karl with special challenges and opportunities. Since his father's name was Noel, this was an all-out celebration every year. Karl would get so excited we learned to control the momentum of the holiday by limiting the activities and decorating, beginning the 12th day before Christmas. Each day would be enhanced with one activity: baking, Christmas cards, tree decorating, wrapping presents, etc. Eventually, Karl decorated his own tree and named it the "Hallelujah Tree."

Karl shopped at our local Dollar Store, selecting wonderful and appropriate gifts. One amazing selection took place in 2008. The financial world had collapsed in September. Brett, Laura's husband, was in financial services, and Karl selected a toilet bowl candle as his gift.

Over the years, Karl's travels became quite elaborate. There was the five-stop Southwest Airlines trip to Toledo, Ohio, to see his Godfather. Karl loved the take off and landings. Then there was the cruise ship where he loved the "fancy food" and meeting the captain with a snappy salute. A weekend in Las Vegas prompted, "I *LIKE* this place." There were two trips to North Carolina's outer banks, and ultimately a two-week trip to Ireland and Scotland where he celebrated his 39th birthday in a charming old hotel with twenty-some church friends, "Whew, that was a long trip home."

All in all, Karl learned to be flexible, and so did those around him. New sights and experiences gave him the joy of anticipation and the pleasure of remembering. He would "pour" over pictures from every trip and could share a long-forgotten moment complete with a twinkle in his eye.

Karl at 16

Thursday, February 25th, 2010

Because the staff was so accommodating, Noel and I took turns, along with Laura, Karl's Godmother Janis, and occasionally, his brother Michael, staying in his room. This routine was for our benefit, I'm sure, and speaks to the graciousness of the staff. We were deeply appreciative.

About one o'clock, Dr. Rentz, Karl's attending physician came into his room to talk to Laura, Noel, and me. I'll never forget his words. "For all practical purposes, Karl was dead when you brought him into the hospital Tuesday morning. For all practical purposes, he is dead now. All his life functions have been taken over by machines. If he survives, it will be a long drawn out recuperation. I would like to see him walk out of here under his own power, but I can't guarantee that."

While it was a shock and painful to hear, in retrospect, we came to appreciate Dr. Rentz's directness and honesty.

Health is Everything!

Perhaps the greatest challenge facing a parent dealing with a child who has disabilities is working out where *normal* ends and the disability begins. All children have health issues, and all parents have questions about those issues: "Is my child too small, too big, too noisy, too active, too quiet?" Our frames of reference become interactions in the neighborhood, the day care center, the congregation and the playground. Even then, when we begin to be concerned, well-meaning friends and family members remind us that Albert Einstein didn't speak early and actually failed algebra.

My interactions with the professional medical community were interesting and varied. Some physicians would reassure an anxious mother that "each child develops at his own pace" and that "it's most important that you, Mom, relax and allow the baby some space." As I consulted physician after physician, I was looking for the holy grail, a quick fix, a miracle. One plastic surgeon stunned me when he would spin a crystal pendulum and stated I was the "cause" of Karl's problems!

In July of 1978, my mom took Karl to San Antonio for a two-week session with a touch therapist. Another time, in 1995, he was diagnosed as "undifferentiated schizophrenic." And yet, in September of 1996, in a journal entry, I listed Karl as one of the four people I knew who I considered "content" with their situation in life.

As time progressed, it became apparent Karl was not developing normally, either physically or mentally, and his physical ailments were occurring too frequently and were relatively severe. In addition, his hyperactivity was uncontrollable.

Many a night as a young child he would be up for hours tearing the pantry apart. Without medication, I couldn't deal with him. With medication, I worried about side effects and long term consequences, although at the time, I have to confess, the here and now was far more important than the long term. Because of Ritalin, Karl's growth pattern was quite stunted, perhaps because of medication; perhaps because of his hyperactivity.

He had to visit the hospital on such a routine basis that he would grab the steering wheel when we drove past that corner so I couldn't turn into the hospital driveway. We were open to trying everything available. I had consulted several doctors to little avail. By the time Karl was four, I refused to allow any more tests or blood samples. I had decided that we were going to accept this situation and make the best of it.

Yet, from his mid-teens, when he outgrew Ritalin (or Melaril or Thorazine), until his late twenties, Karl's health remained pretty stable, and he led a relatively normal life, participating in work, social activities, and sports events.

When his health began to deteriorate, I failed to see the pattern. Each time, he was able to "come around," and we just continued living, looking forward to the next trip or family gathering. He was always a good patient, willing to rest on the couch so I could keep an eye on him. He was willing to take the medications that might help him recover. He was willing to push himself to be a part of the world around him.

He suffered from headaches and hiccups. Sometimes he would move his hand in front of his eyes as if he was seeing double, and he had an amazing variety of strategies to get rid of his hiccups.

Health is everything. Between care, encouragement and pure will power, one can overcome many health weaknesses.

March 2010, Keeping a Log...

Even though time has passed, the events of March 2010 are vivid. Laura suggested we begin a log tracking Karl's vital signs and progress. This was a great strategy because the mind can easily forget and/or fudge the details.

The nightmare from February 24th to March 2nd had included a respirator and Karl being placed completely on life support. The log actually begins on March 2, Texas Independence Day.

By March 2nd, the respirator had been removed, and Karl was able to breath on his own. A speech therapist was scheduled to check his throat to see if he was able to eat. Hopefully, he would begin with pureed food, slowly progressing to real *chewing* food. The pulmonologist who looked at Karl's X-rays was not happy with the sound of his throat. Later in the day, Dr. Patel, the cardiologist, stopped by and said Karl looked more alert. Karl shook his hand. The steroids were reduced from 100 to 75 to help reduce the high insulin count of 297.

March 3rd, a physician became aware that Karl's adrenals gland may not be working. He did eat a teaspoon of egg and a teaspoon of banana. When the physical therapist came to help him sit on the side of the bed, his blood pressure registered 175/119.

March 4th, his vital signs spiked again with a heart rate of 143 and a blood pressure reading of 166/109. Of even greater concern was a gurgling in his throat that got continually worse. At 7:00 pm., Noel helped the nurse clear the mucus. For the first time since the tube had been removed, Karl slept quietly all night long!

No one seemed able to determine the cause of Karl's problems. No culture results were ever determined. The vagueness was very disorienting. When he would swallow, he coughed. Meanwhile the congestion persisted and his lungs had to be suctioned on a regular basis. An IV was started and antibiotics administered continually as a prophylactic. A nurse reported the speech therapist checked his throat and recommended no feeding by mouth until he was stronger.

And so it went, day by excruciating day. We were on six-hour shifts now, days and nights melting into one another. With his medical background, Noel knew Karl's situation was precarious. All I could say to family members was, "Hug your children and tell them how much you love them."

A Silent Tear

Pass the hospital where you recovered
A silent tear rolls down my cheek
Torn between the
Pain of remembering
And the
Fear of forgetting.
A silent tear of memory.

—Susan Giesecke
July 13, 2012

SAN DIEGO, it's all about Perspective...

When life presents you with lemons,
make lemonade!

The ability to laugh is a gift.

In 1977 we decided to take a vacation in southern California. Disneyland, Knott's Berry Farm and the San Diego Zoo were the big attractions drawing us to this area. Noel's family had always taken extensive vacations because of his father's work. They would be gone for as much as six weeks at a time. Many times, Curtis, Noel's father, would work for three of those weeks; then vacation for the remaining three weeks.

We flew to Los Angeles, spent three days at Disneyland, then drove to San Diego to see the Zoo and the beach. In between, Karl and I shared a trip to the Crystal Cathedral in Thousand Oaks, California. It had started as a drive-in church in the 50s, and became a phenomenal congregation, perhaps the beginning of the mega-church movement. The cathedral was immense, and the service bordered on being a Hollywood production. We enjoyed a cab ride from our Penny Motel, and we loved every minute of the ride and the church service.

But the highlight of the trip was our outing to the beach. By this time, Karl was taking some relatively strong medications, Ritalin 25 mg. three times a day. The day of our outing to the beach was perfect San Diego weather. San Diego needs no air-conditioning. We learned that when Noel had me call the desk clerk of the motel to ask how to turn on the air-conditioning. "Madam, there is no need for air-conditioning in San Diego." And that was true.

We were within walking distance of the beach. When we arrived, Laura and Kevin ran into the water to play while Michael stayed with us. About an hour into our time there, I noticed Karl was standing on a raised area and twirling around and around, as he was prone to do, particularly when the medication began to wear off.

Even more interesting was the group of young people next to the street watching Karl. At first, I thought they were watching Karl because they thought him weird, but as I watched, I realized there was more going on. They were amazed and impressed. This was the era of the drug culture and these kids were obviously druggies. Noel and I had to laugh when we realized that Karl *off* drugs achieved the high those druggies wanted. And he got his drugs legally!

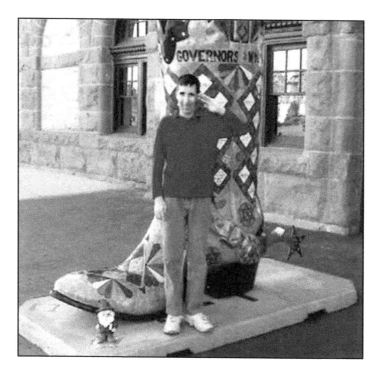

Karl in Wyoming 2004

Monday, March 8, 2010

Be kind to everyone you meet because
he or she is also enduring a great struggle

This litany of daily activities recalls the heroic effort expended by the professionals and family members during these very trying days of overwhelming and ongoing challenges.

Monday, March 8th, Karl sat himself up and the physical therapy folks stood him up. He said he was dizzy. When he jumped back in bed, he lay on his side, and when he opened his eyes, you could tell he was exhausted.

Tuesday, March 9th, he sat in a chair for an hour. Dr. Rance wanted him to pass the swallow test before moving to a Select Specialty Hospital. Later, Karl was administered the barium test. He was too weak to swallow and would need a feeding tube inserted so he could get some nutrition.

Wednesday, March 10th, the insertion could not be performed because Karl's blood pressure numbers were terrible. He had hyper-ventilated and the blood gases were unacceptable. Oxygen and steroids were restored immediately.

The following week was a series of ups and downs of coughing and blood pressure issues, requiring suctioning and lots of breathing treatments.

Sunday, March 14th, Dr. Rance thought Karl was doing better and encouraged the Wii, a computer game system Karl loved. Kevin was in town and set it up. Karl looked so good playing games, we took pictures that Laura sent out to the many friends and relatives who were keeping him close in thought and prayer.

Tuesday, March 16th, the "peg" was inserted. At 4:00, he received his first "feeding" to see if he tolerated the new feeding routine.

Wednesday, March 17th, a nurse reported a fever during the night.

Friday, March 19th, he was back on the IV because he could not absorb enough nutrients to support himself.

Monday, March 22nd, Karl moved to Select, a therapy hospital. He'd walked 50 feet! I stood there crying as I watched his skinny legs support his fragile body. At Select, the foley tube was removed. A speech therapist tried the swallow test and Karl aspirated.

Saturday, March 27th, he aspirated during the night and became very sick. His heart rate rose to 170s and 180s. He was lethargic all day, and the congestion continued. The pic line was removed to check for infection.

<u>Monday, March 29th</u>, we were told there was an abnormal culture, and for the first time we had a hint what Karl was facing!

<u>Wednesday, March 31st</u>, we celebrated, because Karl sat up in a chair for an hour.

By April 2nd, the "infection" was under control. The heart doctor said Karl's heart rate was slow and occasionally arrythmatic. Dr. Rance was still concerned with Karl aspirating. Dr. Lee felt the constant battle was to keep Karl's lungs clear.

Special Olympics Motto:

I pledge to do my best to win.
If I cannot win,
Let me be brave in the attempt.

Next to the ancient Greeks, no society has placed more emphasis on sports and competition that ours. And who would argue against the positive benefits of exercise and challenge?

By the time we had consulted several professionals, we learned that the professionals were really guiding us to learn to accept, to deal with, and to help our Karl. One of the psychologists encouraged games and puzzles as a strategy, and we mastered 50- and 100-piece puzzles. At first, I was quite skeptical of games, thinking of them more as a diversion and play rather than an end in themselves. Over time, however, I realized the benefits. Games *can* help in relationship development, in learning to live within the rules, and in providing some structure and order to play activity.

As important as the individual and parent/child work was participation in the Special Olympics. Beginning in the early 60s, Eunice Shriver, of the Kennedy family, because of her own sister, Rose Marie, saw how unfairly people with intellectual disabilities were treated. She became the catalyst behind the Special Olympics, a program designed for persons with an IQ of 70 or less to participate in athletic events on a competitive basis.

41

The Special Olympics help build self-esteem and physical development from which participants derive feelings of success as well as learning to accept defeat.

This organization is truly special with amazing stories flowing from the competitions. Athletes would stop mid-race to help a fellow athlete who had stumbled. The winning added an entirely new component. Karl participated, through the school district in many Special Olympics activities. During one basketball game, he scored the first basket for his team, and his joy was unbounded. He celebrated a full five minutes, then he proceeded to score 16 of the team's winning 29 points. What a thrill! That one game gave Karl a unique sense of accomplishment as well as his once-in-a-lifetime fifteen minutes of fame.

Another experience, however, had a different lesson to teach us. It was a swim meet in San Antonio, and the athletes were staying on a college campus, living in the dorms. Late one evening, a counselor called to tell us the group had gone on an outing to a local shopping center and she was calling to report that Karl had been gone from the group for an hour and half. They had looked everywhere and felt it was time to let us know what had happened.

I was stunned, and the situation provoked a study in crisis management in our family. As I told Noel, Karl's father, he continued to work on a dental crown he was carving. Kevin, who was still living at home at the time, wanted to get into his car and drive to San Antonio immediately to look for Karl himself. After 20 minutes, I decided to call by brother, who lived in San Antonio and was active in the real estate industry, to ask for his help and advice. An hour later, the counselor called back to say that all was well. Karl had apparently missed the bus going to the shopping center, and they found him asleep in bed when they returned to the dorms.

Another favorite sport of Karl's was the six-week Annual Baseball Tournament sponsored by the local Optimists Club. Interestingly, a patient of Noel's began the program many years prior to Karl's participation. Little did we know how much this program would come to mean to so many people. All Special Education students were eligible, especially those long since graduated from high school. Teams were chosen and given shirts each year. Each game lasted one hour. Participants batted until they hit the ball, and the enjoyment and the camaraderie were shared by siblings, parents, and players alike. No one particularly cared who won, and everyone cheered when a runner crossed home plate. Soft drinks marked the end of the game and a banquet at IHOP marked the end of the season.

Each participant brought a spirit of hope to the plate, imitating professional ball players' stances and swings. The race around the diamond brought everyone into the game. "Go back to first! We can't have three people on 3rd!" The Optimist Club members kept the rules while preserving the spirit of the game. Once you moved into this world, you no longer watched athletic events without observing and celebrating a great pass, an amazing basket, a base-loaded home run, regardless of team affiliation.

Many times, even now, as we attend a sporting event, I find myself jumping up and down cheering enthusiastically. My companion will remind me I'm cheering for the *wrong* team, and I'll stop, stunned, and say, "It's my Special Olympics background. I'm cheering for the great play someone just made and the courage of the players." Who wins has become immaterial. The "game" is the thing.

Special Olympics with best friend Michael Machac

Once

Once he breathed, swallowed, walked and talked
With effort, to be sure
Yet, assumed and expected

Now: no assumptions, no expectations

Then: still hope, grace, love and acceptance

When normal becomes abnormal:
Stunned shock, despair, discouragement and depression

Then the questions: Why, how, when, what does this mean?

Finally, it is what it is.
What do I need to know?
How do we do?
How do we survive?

Celebrate: When there is life, there is hope!

- -Susan Giesecke
March 29, 2010

45

Karl at the Lake on Easter

Working, Really?

In an effort to maintain a *normal* life, Karl was expected to work, to be a contributing member of the community and society.

The school district also promoted this concept, so the years before graduation provided a wide variety of employment opportunities. This process began with a questionnaire:

1. Do you like to work with people or alone?
2. Indoors or outdoors?
3. Daytime or evening?

Finding the right work situation was a challenge. It needed to be close, be *doable* for him, have willing supervisors. It also needed to fit into the family's ability to support with bus or physical transportation. Some paid employment worked, and some didn't.

Karl's first work experience was at home. He was an amazing dental towel folder. His stack was beautifully layered, and his performance was always prompt. He earned $4.00 each week.

One of his most memorable work experiences was at Wendy's. Karl would ride the local bus back and forth, a great step toward independence. In addition to cleaning and emptying

the wastebaskets, he would help behind the counter, delivering orders and taking drinks to the patrons sitting in the dining area.

After several months, I realized Karl wasn't going to work. It was a few days before I could connect with the manager and learned he would not be working at Wendy's any longer. Being a take charge kind of Mom, I asked what had happened, only to learn from the manager that when Karl delivered drinks to a table, the customer asked, "Which of the two drinks was the Coke?" Karl promptly picked each drink up, tasted it, and said, "This one is the Coke."

On another occasion, the earnest manager said, Karl did not dispose of the garbage appropriately.

Wendy's had a wood enclosed garbage area behind the restaurant, requiring the opening of a door and the placement of the garbage in the bin. Karl would apparently swing the garbage over the fenced-in area, rather than open the available door. As the manager delivered this news, I was sympathetic, but laughing so hard on the inside it was all I could do to get out the door and into my car.

Karl's final work experience, for pay, was at Albertson's, a nationwide grocery chain. All went well. Karl was a good and energetic worker. One day, Orlando, the supervisor, contacted me to say, "Karl does not need to sweep the front of the entire 12 store shopping center and he does not need to get the grocery cart from the middle of the busy street in front of the grocery store."

All in all, his paid employment was a gift. Karl enjoyed saving and spending his earnings. After a half year's work, he bought a remote-control truck, a ticket to see David Copperfield, a season ticket to the opera and an airline ticket to San Antonio.

After Albertson's closed the doors on our local store, a new grocery chain took over the property. I suggested to Karl that he may want to work at the new grocery. He was emphatic, "No way. It's too complicated. People leave their carts and cars in the no parking zones. They do not mind."

All in all, the school districts put great effort into job skill development and placement. In the real world, however, we found full-time employment virtually impossible to maintain.

So, in addition to paid positions, a number of volunteer opportunities were explored: a local food pantry, a local nursing home, organizing gift cards for a non-profit, preparing shoebox kits for seafarers stranded in Houston during Christmas and Lutheran World Relief school kits. This kept Karl busy and involved in the community.

Ultimately, Karl chose to volunteer at Terrace Elementary, a school half a block from the house. A former Special Education teacher was now principal and securing an opportunity for three hours a day was possible. I had long waged a verbal battle with the system: Why do we work so hard to encourage our family members to have acceptable work skills when there are no jobs available in the community for them? Even organizations like (MHMRA) Mental Health and Rehabilitation Administration had no developmentally challenged employees.

Karl's three hours a day at Terrace Elementary spanned a wide variety of activities: custodial helper assistant, library shelf duster, helping little children clear lunch trays and emptying wastebaskets. To each he brought a level of dedication and seriousness admired by many, especially the Special Education class in the second grade. All people can be valued contributors to society at some level.

One year, Karl's name was placed on the school's outdoor marquis for his birthday. Another year his birthday was celebrated by a luncheon provided by the teachers and staff. One of the biggest thrills of Karl's life was his induction as the 2006 PTA Lifetime Member, complete with cheers, a pin and a plaque. He was devoted to Terrace Elementary. Barbara, his at-school Mom, along with the entire staff, kept him challenged and interested.

Through all the efforts at employment, one of Karl's biggest challenges was my learning to recognize the need to change and learning to let go. It is so easy to be over-protective of a special needs family member. Ultimately I learned that when Karl acted out, he was trying to tell me he needed a new challenge, a new learning. Mismatched expectations. The challenge of separating his disability from normal developmental states was always perplexing.

In 2003 Karl announced he needed a scooter to get to school. By this time, we had moved about a mile from the school and the walk could be a challenge. When he got the scooter, we were faced with crossing a busy street, other vehicles on the sidewalk as well as walkers who "would not mind." After a couple of semi-serious falls, Karl decided a small model of a scooter was "better than a real one."

One Wednesday, Karl announced, "Only two more days until the weekend!" Later, upon sharing the line with his brother Michael, who was working full time. Michael responded,

"Weekend? He's volunteering, right? Three hours a day, right?"
And *he's* looking forward to the weekend?"

Happy Birthday Karl – at Terrace Elementery

Sunday, April 4, 2010
Easter Sunday

Sunday, April 4, While the Christian world celebrated, Karl sustained so much coughing, he was suctioning himself. His weight was down to 99.3 pounds.

Tuesday, April 6, Dr. Lee mentioned Karl will always be at risk for infections.

The following week was filled with therapy, medications and suctioning secretions.

Tuesday, April 13th, Karl dressed in pajamas and went to the gym to play ball. His heart rate went up so high he was returned to his room. He did sit up in a chair from 10:45 until 1:00. Even at 7:25 p.m., his pulse was still 117.

Wednesday, April 15th, He had another coughing spell which prompted a new EEG and Chest X-Ray.

Thursday, April 16th, Karl's heart rate rose to 130, so physical therapy was postponed.

Sunday and Monday, April 19th and 20th, First there was
the barium test and Karl was not able to swallow and required
suctioning. The next day, Karl had vomited, and his bedding was
in complete disarray. There was no physical therapy because
Karl's heart rate was registering at 130-150.

Thursday, April 23rd, He started coughing and throwing up
food. Later in the day, Karl was moved to Heartland. Heartland
was a therapy and long-term care facility. I selected it because it
was located between Laura and us. As it turned out, some of our
friends had placed their beloved family members there in the
past. All the physical therapy staff was outstanding. Two other
young men Karl's age lived there: Paul, 41, and Richard, 44.
They were both severely physically disabled, yet verbally
coherent, pleasant young men.

During the intake/evaluation process, Karl weighed in at 90
pounds. Part of the planning raised questions like, "What does
Karl need to achieve to go home? Do you have a Plan B? Here
are your options… assisted living, etc."

Friday, May 1st, Karl's weight had dropped to 87.4 pounds,
and he began coughing a great deal the following day. When he
would sit up straight the coughing ceased.

Thursday, May 7th, We noticed Karl was losing a lot of
hair.

Friday, May 8th, An issue developed over Karl's food on
May 8, and his weight dropped to 86.8.

One scene stays vividly in my mind: Each day the speech therapist would come to Karl's room. She entered with a smile of encouragement. I would welcome her, excited for a break in the routine. Karl, however, was a bit more apprehensive. The exercises, I'm sure, were difficult for him. Speech had never been his strong suit, even before the respirator and swallowing issues developed.

The therapist had a set of twelve exercises repeated three times each. Karl, wanting her approval, really worked hard to repeat each exercise successfully.

When they reached the final exercise, a practice of o's and g's, Karl would look her in the eyes and say "g, g, go, go home!"

"When we sing, we breathe together..."

The power/gift of music is rare and beautiful. Karl knew that power and had the gift. Of his many gifts, music was by far the most important love of his life.

His musical interest was inspired by a neighbor who invested 30 minutes a day, as a part of her own recovery program, patiently teaching Karl at age 10, piano chords and tunes. He later successfully studied piano with a private instructor for over 12 years.

This love of music grew into an extensive collection of musical instruments and CD's covering all types of music, except country and western. He taught himself to play many instruments and was gifted at improvisation.

In addition, Karl and I became "culture buddies," frequenting the Houston ballet, the opera and symphony scene, as well as Irish dance, the Turkish festival and International Festivals.

As we would travel, we'd pick up hand-me-down instruments at the second-hand stores, have them refurbished and rebuilt at our local music store and share them with Karl. Also, friends and family would pass on practice instruments. Karl would save his money from work and from doing chores around the house to buy an instrument. I am reminded of the flugelhorn he purchased after three years of saving.

On any given day, one might hear strains of guitar, organ, clarinet, or piccolo trumpet waft down the stairs. I often imagined that an "angel" lived upstairs because the melodies could be hauntingly beautiful. As he took professional lessons, one recital brought tears to my eyes, the music was so well presented.

His professional teacher, Eileen, was at first reluctant to teach Karl, because of his learning disabilities, but when her husband suffered brain damage from a terrible car accident, Eileen offered to *try* Karl as a student. The two became fast friends. While Karl's progress was slower than most, his dedication was impressive. Other students would be told, "Karl does this technique…," and they would work to rise to the challenge.

In 1980, we attended our first Houston Symphony performance together and Karl loved every minute of it. A few months later, I told Karl, "We have an extra ticket to an upcoming performance. Would you like to invite a friend or a teacher to join us?" After a long pause, he replied, "Mom, not many people in my class like classical music." I told him not to worry, not many of my friends understood classical music either.

Over the years we attended many performances together. The Houston cultural scene was booming, and we relished it all. A special relationship developed between Karl and a distant cousin, Jeff Butler, a cellist in the Houston Symphony. Jeff respected Karl's musical abilities and truly treated him as a fellow musician. One time, Karl played a tune on the harmonica and Jeff named it. Was Karl impressed! Another time Jeff gave Karl a cello lesson and commented that he had the perfect cello posture and a great natural vibrato. In honor of Karl's 40th birthday, Jeff and Wendy Smith Butler, his wife and a professional cellist as well, played a duet at church. It was beautiful, and Karl was ecstatic.

Karl performed at several family weddings. I would read the II Corinthians passage—the love chapter, and he would accompany me on a soprano recorder. When I would suggest he practice, he'd say that wasn't necessary.

Hans Kung, a prominent Catholic theologian once said, "Music is the window through which we see God." While intellectually you can study the physics of sound and the mathematics of performance, there is that leap of faith when science and art combine to create the magic that touches your heart and soul. Musicians know the joy of making music, both individually and as an ensemble.

"When we sing, we breathe together…"

Karl at a piano recital

"Don't Stop the Music, Let's Dance!"

Have you heard of Fred Astaire and Ginger Rogers? Put them on the far side of a continuum, and I'll describe the pair that makes them look so good.

About every five years, Karl and I would get the urge to learn to dance. He was good at rhythm and I loved to dance as well. Our first effort was devoted to hip hop, which was fashionable at the time. It had a great beat and required active physical involvement on our part. I liked the idea of hip hop because it could help Karl build self-confidence in the performance of intricate steps. In addition, he could participate with others, particularly family members, at outings. And it offered a great opportunity to connect mental commands with body actions.

We discovered Leisure Learning, who offered 6 classes, an hour each, on consecutive Tuesday evenings.

As we drove to the class with me in my business attire, I never dreamed we would be stretching full legged at one minute and hopping backward the next. Tentatively we opened the door to the class to discover 18 beautiful young people dressed in appropriate active wear.

Not to be discouraged, Karl and I tried to be good sports. Karl really tried to accurately execute the moves. Our beats were broke and our rhythm a bit off time, but our enthusiasm never waned.

Our second venture into the world of dance, after a five-year recovery, was tap dancing. This time we utilized the Adult Education program of our local school district. When we arrived, armed with new tap shoes, we were greeted by 15 ladies who had been studying level 1 for four consecutive years.

Karl had been watching movies of Fred Astaire, an amazing dancer, and we had visions of performing as a duo for the family. The intricacies of a simple tap routine are amazing: "Step, step, together, whish, whish, slide." And to music! Again, we were the bookends age-wise and truly the beginners. Nevertheless, our desire overcame these obstacles and we practiced as if we were on our way to stardom.

Our final effort in the world of dance was salsa. Living in Texas, Latin music is everywhere, ranchero and meringue, among others. Utilizing the opportunity of the school district again, we signed up for a semester. I can still see the expression on the face of our charming salsa teacher when we walked into the class—late, as usual. The teacher was a wonderful dancer and a patient teacher. He would count out the eight beats of the salsa rhythm, moving his hips, ever so Latin. It was a beautiful sight and inspiring to those of us in the class.

And we tried. Oh, how we tried! Learning the step backward, as a partner, was a real challenge. Never to be discouraged, though, we attended every class, picturing ourselves as the Fred and Ginger of salsa. At the end of the day, I had to admit the spirit was willing, but the flesh was weak. And the teacher, rather than having the class dance at the recital, chose to invite an outside dancing partner to demonstrate the salsa to the audience!

As I write these words, I'm remembering our joy at learning something new and popular. We had fun and we proved that everyone can enjoy dancing.

May 2010: Encouraging...

The following week was encouraging. Karl was able to maintain his "numbers" without oxygen. On Mother's Day, Karl shared some private thoughts with Laura.

Saturday, May 16th: Karl's weight climbed to 89.4, an almost 3-pound increase and today he walked the entire hall behind a wheelchair.

Sunday, May 17th: In the evening, Serkin, Ayse, and the entire Ceylon family visited. The Ceylon family is from Turkey, and we created a memorable evening at the Heartland Care facility, locating an empty room for our guests to observe prayers.

Monday, May 18th: After almost three months, the port was removed.

Wednesday, May 20th: Rene Renquist from Texas Lutheran University visited while Noel was with Karl, and Kevin came to visit. The two played Wii for four hours. Karl's weight: 91 pounds!

Sunday, May 24th: Once again, Karl was unable to pass the barium test. He aspirated. Everyone was so discouraged I began to plan to learn to live with this new reality in our lives. We were hearing stories of people who lived with feeding tubes for years, successfully. The staff at Heartland, however, regrouped and intensified Karl's therapy: physical, occupational and speech.

A great development was the discovery of a piano in the dining room on the second floor and the opportunity for Karl to practice, so each day began to fall into a routine. He had therapies in the morning. Laura would show up at noon and spend time with him. I would arrive about 2:30 so Laura and I could visit before she had to leave. Noel would arrive about 6:00 so we could share a meal together. Then he would stay to "tuck Karl in" at 9:00 p.m. These days were blessed in many ways. Each of us had a schedule of activities with Karl that we enjoyed.

Wednesday, May 27th: Karl answered the phone when I called in the morning. We had a good visit. His weight was up a whole pound!

Sunday, May 31st: We watched *Fisherman's Almanac*, Kevin's Careco show. At the end, Wade, the host said, "Fishing has been so good, even the cameraman is fishing!" and they showed Kevin. We were so excited, and it was fun to tell Kevin we saw him on TV.

One strategy we enjoyed each day was for me to assemble a paper airplane. Noel's sister Barbara gave Karl a Christmas gift of a *Day by Day Paper Airplane Calendar*. After I would get the day's plane assembled, which was not always an easy thing to do, Karl would fly it, trying to get it to go out the door of the hospital room. On Memorial Day, Karl's paper airplane went out the door and landed in the middle of the hall. What an exciting day!

The next week, Karl was moved to Bolos feeding, so he was freed of the tower and the feeding apparatus. It also meant he could use the port-a-potty and wear tennis shoes. His weight was constantly improving: 92.6 to 95 in one week.

Sunday, June 16th: Now that he was free of external tubes, we were finally able to go out. We went to Christ the King for Saturday evening worship and then to Holy Cross on June 16. These were special occasions indeed. Miracles as far as I was concerned.

Monday, June 24th: Karl was moved from the second floor to room 1203 on the newly renovated first floor. We still went upstairs for piano practice. We were inspired to practice a duet to play for Holy Cross. It was Karl's favorite hymn, #611, "I Heard the Voice of Jesus Say." It was a hymn used for healing. We called it the Scottish Hymn.

Ephesians 5: 18b-20

...Be filled with the spirit, addressing one another with
psalms and hymns and spiritual songs, singing and making
melody to the Lord with all your heart, always and for everything
giving thanks in the name of our Lord Jesus Christ to God the Father.

If ever this passage was true, our religious community, Holy Cross Lutheran, was living proof. Karl was baptized at Holy Cross and remained an active participant throughout, from Sunday School classes to Handbell Choir. His faith seemed to be a central part of his existence.

A traditional custom in our family is the table prayer before meals. We prayed Martin Luther's simple table prayer:

> *Come, Lord Jesus, be our guest.*
> *Let these gifts to us be blessed.*

In addition to the obvious spiritual dimension, prayer allows everyone time to take a deep breath, relax, and prepare for our mealtime together.

As a young child, probably about 12, with all six family members around the table, Karl began the prayer before any other member of the family. After a few words, it was obvious to all, he was struggling. Soon, everyone was joining Karl to complete the prayer. I thought anew: *When we pray together, we breath together.*

He was also very matter of fact about death. When I'd tell him the news of a friend's or relative's passing, he'd simply nod his head, as if to say, "this, too, is a part of life."

During Karl's confirmation years, Gene Fogt, our pastor at the time, came to our home to teach Karl privately. One day, Karl announced he would like to be an acolyte, a role traditionally performed by confirmation students. After six weeks of practice with a pool stick (complete with a paper attachment to approximate the lighter attachment/dimmer at the end) as a candle lighter and the piano bench as alter, Karl assisted at services. What a red-letter day! Gene Fogt's reponse, "Would that all our acolytes served with such dedication and enthusiasm!"

As the years rolled by, the variety of Karl experiences at Holy Cross continued: he played "Amazing Grace" on the harmonica for the congregation's 40th anniversary, ushered with his Dad, volunteered at the Food Pantry, worked at the Garage Sale, and played Congo drums for the contemporary worship service.

He loved to greet people at the Fellowship Hall door. If he especially liked you, he would hold the door shut until you recognized him and returned his smile. One pastor said, "Karl forced you to stop for just a minute to reflect…"

Finally, he settled into his favorite activities: playing the G4 in the Handbell Choir and playing his harmonica during communion services. He was lovingly referred to as the congregation's "favorite son" or "mascot."

Holy Cross Lutheran Sanctuary, *taken by Bede Van Dyke*

July 2010: Recovery!

Hymn #611: "I Heard the Voice of Jesus Say"

I heard the voice of Jesus say, "Come unto Me and rest;
Lay down, thou weary one, lay down Thy head upon My breast."
I came to Jesus as I was, weary and worn and sad;
I found in Him a resting place, and He has made me glad.

I heard the voice of Jesus say, "Behold I freely give
The living water; thirsty one, stoop down, and drink and live."
I came to Jesus, and I drank of that life-giving stream;
My thirst was quenched, my soul revived, and now I live in Him.

I heard the voice of Jesus say, I am this dark world's Light;
Look unto Me, thy morn shall rise, and all the day be bright."
I looked to Jesus, and I found in Him my Star, my Sun;
And in that light of life I'll walk, till traveling days are done.

I wrote two variations on the hymn. I played the base, and Karl played the treble. We had a great time practicing. Members of the staff would stop by to listen and were quite complimentary.

Karl was moved from the second floor to the first floor, Room 1203, with a private shower. He said, "This is like an apartment." And one afternoon, we went to the monthly birthday party where there was a Disc Jockey. This is Progress!

The month of July was such fun. Karl was feeling well, so we went to church, shopping, taking piano lessons and visiting family.

Friday, July 2nd: Karl passed the infamous swallow test!

Saturday, July 3rd: Kevin came to visit and on the 4th of July, Karl's dear friends, Jeff Cordes and his family, drove from San Antonio to spend the afternoon.

Saturday, July 10th: Karl's weight is moving up daily hitting 101.1 today. By now we are listening to *The Greek Hero* lectures from The Teaching Company and we are inspired by their courage. Our favorites were Achilles and Agamemnon.

Wednesday, July 21st: By the 21st, Karl graduated from Occupational Therapy and Physical Therapy, complete with an oversized T-shirt to prove it.

July 17th was circus day, and on August 1st Karl moved home. What a day of celebration! We played our duet in church for the congregation, then moved home. Cousin Pam was there to help straighten Karl's room in his upstairs apartment. What a collector he was! We collected 8 huge black contractor bags which we took to the attic for storage so his room looked presentable. Then we moved him home and upstairs. Now we had a whole new set of collections and treasures to incorporate into the house.

It had been a long ordeal. The miracle occurred, and we were incredibly grateful.

The Love of My Life...

How do I love, you, let me count the ways...
—Elizabeth Barrett Browning (Sonnet 43)

As we were expressing our care and concern for Karl, he was carrying on a very vivid and active love life too.

In 1991 our family held the first extended family reunion in Dubuque, Iowa. There, Karl laid eyes on Cousin Claudia, mother of an infant 19 months old, and fell utterly and totally in love. Claudia became Karl's ultimate imaginary friend, confidant and companion from then on. Hundreds of pictures were created of Claudia. They were everywhere—carefully constructed into frames, (handmade, of course), photo albums, key chains, wall hangings, notebooks and folders.

Claudia knew she was beloved but probably didn't appreciate the full extent until she and her family vacationed in Texas one Spring Break and spent a night in our home. The look of total devotion in Karl's eyes was one small clue of his unconditional love.

Karl experienced one date with a real live girl named Christine. Following that experience, he found paper women his forte, specifically Princess Diana, Marilyn Monroe, and Princess Leah.

What followed was an impressive library of books related to the Princesses and Marilyn. Ultimately, three cardboard cut-outs shared his bedroom—and bed. When I'd wake him in the morning, one of the "statues" would greet me, flat out on her side of his bed.

Most telling were his brothers who were impressed and rather envious of Karl's love interests. These "women" went to bed when he wanted them and never talked back!

In addition, Princess Leah collected an elaborate array of nurse's coverings, complete with syringes and pockets for stethoscopes. This was a good idea because her Star Wars costume was skimpy, to say the least.

One January, we assembled a very complicated puzzle of Marilyn Monroe: ten images, in varying stages of dress and undress, and a signature. I thought the project hopeless—750 pieces, but after three weeks and untold hours, Karl placed the final piece. We had the puzzle framed, and it still hangs over his bed.

Love of Karl's life!

August 2010: Reborn

Beginning August 1st, a new phase of our existence began, one full of routine wrapped in thankfulness.

We experienced such an awareness of each and every day. We shared warm hugs every morning and every evening! A numbing sensation set in, and we wondered, *Did the past few months really happen? How can we be so at peace now and so distraught so very recently? How do people in war-torn nations and in poverty handle life?*

Our appreciation centered around the blessing of caring physicians, nurses, nursing aids, and physical therapists. And we were smug enough to claim God's special blessing on Karl due to the ardent prayers of "God's warriors."

I composed a list of guidelines for hospital/nursing home stays, designed to help others who might be facing similar situations:

The Layperson's Guide to Hospital Stays

1. Keep a diary/log of daily "vitals" and physicians' comments.
2. Ask questions until you receive answers in language suitable for the lay person.
3. Don't get overwhelmed.
4. Take care of yourself and keep your hands busy.

5. Eat, sleep, live. Take breaks to keep involved in your personal life.
6. Take surprises for the patient daily and set up a routine of activities.
7. Befriend all members of the staff. These folks are your knowledgeable eyes and ears. They know the routine and the system.
8. Check the internet to educate yourself about medical terms and topics.

In addition, we learned much from this experience:

9. Keep your faith.
10. Journal for your own sanity.
11. How our dear family and friends loved and cared for us in creative and heartfelt ways.
12. Life is tenuous and fragile.
13. Getting well is very painful and requires serious work.
14. The desire to get well is paramount.
15. Set up an email group to inform all your friends/family of positive news.
16. Entertain the patient as much as possible. Time can move slowly.
17. Enjoy each other.
18. Adopt an attitude of, "Whatever the doctor tells us to do, we will do," and
19. Get counseling if you feel the need.

As September arrived, Karl had a doctor's appointment with Dr. Rance, his primary care physician. As he presented Dr. Rance with an Award, a cardboard syringe statue, Dr. Rance was visibly touched, and I had tears in my eyes. Karl was whole again. He had energy, and he was involved in his projects every day.

School started. The feeding tube was removed. Music again wafted from the second floor, along with the Wii and the TV. Medications flowed on a regular schedule. Karl was so happy to be home and we were happy too.

His birthday came, along with celebrations at Terrace and at home, quiet, for sure, yet deep in gratitude.

In October, Noel went to Colorado for a week, and Karl and I enjoyed our time at home. We went on an outing to look for a new car, and we found just the right car for our needs.

The following week, Karl left us.

Home is Where the Heart is:
Living Arrangements

As a child, Karl enjoyed camps sponsored by wonderful civic and service organizations. Not only did the camps benefit the campers, they provided a much-needed respite for the related parents and families.

One summer, Karl attended Marbridge Ranch, located outside Austin, Texas. We had heard glowing reports of experiences with animals and the out of doors. It was also a long-term living option and very Texas sounding. Parents were encouraged not to contact their family member as that would be distracting. After three weeks, Karl was ready to come home. He was not an outdoorsman!

Another time, when our home life became particularly stressful, I toured a living facility in Beaumont, Texas. What an eye opener! I came home with renewed determination to make things work at home, and we trudged on. Yet, it was helpful to know there were options, even if we chose not to exercise them.

By the time Karl graduated from high school and because of the focus of the Association for Retarded Citizens (ARC) on independent living, we pursued a group home option. This involved multiple appointments and tests to determine Karl's eligibility.

Once this was satisfied, Karl and I interviewed a group home in the neighborhood. To my surprise and delight, he was quite receptive. "Like camping out," he said when he saw his new room. And his best friend, Michael was going to be his roommate.

During the day, activities were scheduled at a sheltered workshop on the far side of the city. This proved to be an asset because Karl loved the hour-long bus ride each way.

For a year this living arrangement was quite successful. Then Michael decided to move home. The new roommates were not a fit for Karl and before we knew it, he was acting out and required medication, which was administered and frequently increased.

When he would come home for the weekend, we hardly knew him. He was listless and lethargic, not the vibrant enthusiastic young son we knew. It became increasingly difficult to take him back to the house.

Finally, on July 17, 1995, Karl moved home for good. He had experienced the outside world and found his home very appealing. We became three "peas in a pod," so to speak. Laura dubbed him, "House Manager," complete with a list of chores and responsibilities. And, he no longer needed medications.

In 2002, we moved to our present home where the upstairs was designated "Karl's apartment." He loved it and made it his own. The guest room welcomed many guests over the years: college presidents and church bishops as well as international guests from Africa.

Karl's music room housed a collection of about 100 instruments decorating the walls and filling the closet, and his den was composed of an efficiency kitchen, a TV, and a special gift from his brother Kevin, a Williams Comet Pin ball machine.

Saluting at the Cabin: Noel, Kevin and dear friend Carl Bridges

Another salute? Noel, Karl and Carl Bridges

October 23, 2010

We had gone to Seguin Thursday night and enjoyed an evening together at a local restaurant eating Mexican food, a Texas favorite. On Friday, Noel and Karl explored their favorite shops and shared a hamburger. By the afternoon, Karl was asleep, tired. In the night, I noticed his breathing was shallow.

By morning, as I left to attend Board of Regents meetings, I told him I was going to call the doctor as soon as I could. We both knew what that meant. As I said, "I love you," and "Goodbye," he nodded his head.

An hour later, Noel came to get me. Karl was gone. His body was peaceful, and I was able to close his beautiful blue eyes. There are no words to express our sense of loss and grief.

What Does it mean to be "creative?"

"Give Karl a piece of cardboard, some string and brads and he's in business," said his Dad. This was true. In addition to his love of music and improvisation, the items he could create were amazing.

If being creative means seeing life from a unique perspective, Karl had that perspective. If, because of hearing loss, words and concepts and ideas could be misinterpreted creatively, Karl had that gift too. He created a world of his own, complete with imaginary friends and conversations; battles and wars.

Cardboard rollers from wrapping paper became chimes. A cardboard syringe became an award for his favorite doctor. Many a cardboard pistol, sword or knife graced his room. Once a stereopticon showed up, complete with cardboard double framed pictures.

A family favorite, particularly among the men, was Boob-centration game. Fashioned after our often-used Disney Memory Game, pairs of boobs had been carefully copied, cut and pasted on to cardboard pieces. Not surprisingly, he enjoyed playing this game, all by himself.

The April Fool's Day joke of 1994 was, "Look... April Fools!" The whole family laughed. The sheer pleasure of seeing Karl want to be a part of the day was the point.

Another April Fool's Day, Karl told his Dad his shoes were untied. His Dad responded, "But I'm wearing loafers…"

One June 21st , Karl announced it was the "Birthday of Summer." And, indeed, it was.

When a dear family friend, who loved and taught Karl and Michael simple magic tricks, had hip surgery, he used a cane for several weeks. When Karl saw Warren without a cane, he said to me, "Look, no cane. That's real magic!"

Another time, when Karl was waiting for a shot to examine his kidneys and bladder, he said to me, "This is not a good idea."

Karl's Dad liked to tease him with stories of his own ballet performances and symphony achievements. One afternoon, Karl had had enough and walked upstairs saying, "I'm not going to listen to this anymore." I didn't blame him and couldn't help laughing.

One evening Madison, the first grandchild, was staying with us. While Karl was usually pleasant and patient, her energy and interest in his "stuff" was obviously getting to him. "When is Laura coming to get her?" he inquired.

One afternoon Karl got his hair cut at the local shop. When I appeared to pick him up, the receptionist said, "He's so happy to see his Grandma." To which I replied, "He's older than he looks. I'm his Mom."

In December 1995, Karl announced he'd slept with Mattie, the dog, the night before. "That's fun, isn't it, Karl," I replied. His response, "Suz, (his name for me), it's like sleeping with a stuffed animal."

One of Karl's first verbal expressions at the age of 5 was asking for a "Doke."

He saw my new dotted swiss housecoat as "snow."

When Karl would be around other disabled or brain damaged children, he noticed. One day, after 6 hours with a dear young friend, Karl stated, "Man, that kid has problems. He has real problems. He needs a hearing aid."

One breakfast, Karl ordered an egg. "How?" asked the waitress. "Hot," he replied.

When his father and the hunting buddies would prepare to go hunting, Karl was invited to join them for a beer because, "I'm 21 now, you know."

Going to Galveston was fun because he got to ride a "boogie board."

One evening the two of us took in a spiritual advisor giving a lecture. On the way home, Karl asked, "Who was that guy?" As I tried to explain, Karl's response was, "He needs to go out and get a job, a *real* job."

A favorite expression of Karl's for several years was, "Perfect."

> How was your day? Perfect.
> How did you sleep? Perfect.
> How was school? Perfect.

We should all be so blessed.

Karl with Pastor Antionette of Cameroon

I Am…

Wounded, shot through my whole by a hole
That does not heal
Never reclaimed to original wholeness.
The pain never ceases.

People say it will get better,
It'll never go away, but "it" will get "better."
What does that mean? "It"? The pain? The memory?
The "change" from then to now?
Better? Than the past? The now?

I'm told you emerge from grief a different person.
I don't know if I want to be different
I don't know if I want to forget.

Yet I have urges to run away, start over, escape.
As a new now emerges, I ask,
Can a wounded whole with a hole exist? Survive?

I am wound tight, full of emotion,
Struggling for space, for light, for air,
Stretching, searching, scanning
The horizon for a place.

—Susan Giesecke
December 21, 2012

There's a Hole in my Heart, Lord

Tell me a heart bearing a hole can be whole
Tell me there is hope and love is worth the cost of pain

My tears are endless and my eyes now dry
My view of the world cynical and rather despairing

After following all the guides for grief, I wonder
How long? When is the magic?

I can't rewind the past to change the pain
I can't imagine the future with a life reframed

What and where is the key?
Is it activity and doing?
Is it passive "being"?
Is it prayer and silence?

Some say time, some say activity
Some say prayer, some say silence

I am at a loss
Vulnerable to depression
Frightened and fearful
Struggling with demons

Devastated by the closing of that volume
Desolate at the final loss of the future of that past

Suspicious of a new future

Afraid I will burst apart and disappear at any moment
Triggered by an unknown something, anything or nothing
Wanting to disappear, to run away, to start over, to change

Yes, the change that comes in life, the inevitable advent of the
future
Now I know a heart can exist with a hole as well as the hope of
wholeness

What is the purpose of a hole?
A hole can provide a view of the future
A hole can allow the planting of a new seed
A hole can be a place to crawl, curl up and recreate
A hole can contain the past in order to layer new experiences
And generate new awareness

It is what it is, yes, and yet…
I do have a choice…
Perhaps that is the real whole!

—Susan
Giesecke
April 25, 2013

Memorials

The Memorial Service honoring Karl's life brought together hundreds of people who had witnessed his life and shared in his challenges. The service opened with Andrew Lloyd Webber's "Pia Jesu" from his *Requiem* and closed with Beethoven's magnificent "Joyful Joyful We Adore Thee." A soloist presented "I Was there to Hear Your Borning Cry" by Jon Yslacker, a popular Lutheran hymn-writer. The words are very special:

> I was there to hear your borning cry,
> I'll be there when you are old.
> I rejoiced the day you were baptized,
> To see your life unfold.
> I was there when you were but a child,
> With a faith to suit you well;
> In a blaze of light you wandered off
> To find where demons dwell.
>
> When you heard the wonder of the Word
> I was there to cheer you on;
> You were raised to praise the living Lord,
> To whom you now belong.
> If you find someone to share your time
> And you join your hearts as one,
> I'll be there to make your verses rhyme
> From dusk to rising sun.

In the middle ages of your life
Not too old, no longer young,
I'll be there to guide you through the night
Complete what I've begun.
When the evening gently closes in,
And you shut your weary eyes,
I'll be there as I have always been
With just one more surprise.

I was there to hear your borning cry,
I'll be there when you are old.
I rejoiced the day you were baptized,
To see your life unfold.

During the service we also sang the hymn Karl and I had played in church on August 1, "I Heard the Voice of Jesus Say."

A music scholarship was established and funded in Karl's name respecting a life well-lived and his love well-shared.

To Lose a Son

I know I'm not alone
My list of friends and acquaintances
Who lost is long.

Be it war, health, accident, suicide
Or murder.

The means are varied;
The result the same.

He is gone.
His spirit a memory.
His loves a gift.

His future is past.

—Susan Giesecke
May 15, 2013

Last Day

One day last week,
Following a medical procedure
I decided to live as if this day was my last.

With a frame around time,
There was no yesterday and no tomorrow.

Only NOW

Only: not as just, but as exclusively!

Each moment gained a specialness,
The colors in the garden vibrant.
My granddaughter's smile, precious beyond words.
And my nighttime bath, luxurious
The day was serendipitous!

"Why," I asked, "is not every day considered my last?"
The feeling was one I truly wanted to last.

—Susan Giesecke
July 9, 2013

My favorite picture of Michael, Laura, Karl and Kevin 2004

Eclipse

The moon, bright and beautiful, has a shadow,
Covering its entire face.
The moon has not changed.
Under the shadow, it is still bright and beautiful.
The shadow came from nowhere
And the moon disappeared.
A mystery!

Sometimes a shadow covers my soul
And my soul disappears; no sight, no light
Underneath, I have not changed.

Watching, slowly the light reappears,
Sliver by sliver
Until the moon is full, bright and beautiful once more.

And so, I too continue on, day by day,
Trusting the light in my soul will return, sliver by sliver.

—Susan Giesecke
October 12, 2014

Karl in 2008

And Now ... The New Now

*The only thing you can take with you
when you're gone, is what you leave behind.*

And now the life, as we experienced it, is over. And yet we struggle to hold onto the experience, to see our loved one in a dream, to assign significance to a fallen feather as a sign. A sign for a memory too rich to be lost, too precious to forget.

So, how do we *honor* a life? How do the simple acts of daily life convey the bond of love? How powerfully we each impact the lives of those around us, those we live with and love.

While the stories shared here are amusing, to be sure, an additional set of stories could reiterate the other side, the pain and suffering of personal hurts caused by careless and thoughtless remarks, the struggle to master the simplest tasks of everyday living and the challenge of maintaining a normal family life.

Could this life and experience help another person, perhaps a family? What is the point of this humble exercise in self-revelation? Are these lessons learned from experience valid and replicable? More important than surviving, have we changed, grown, matured?

Buddhists say, "When the student is ready, the teacher will appear." Along the way, key people and/or statements became significant. For example:

One psychologist helped us to see that our goal was to enable Karl to develop as a person. We learned to be prepared to do whatever it took to accomplish that goal as a family and as parents. It was good advice for all parents and all people, we thought.

The realization that we were not alone went a long way to easing our minds. Perhaps our greatest fear came from the unknown. We were beset by questions such as, "What does this really mean?" and "What should I do now?"

I remember talking with a friend over coffee one morning when Karl was 2 years old, and his hyperactivity was uncontrollable. I was becoming a psychological wreck. "Karl reminds me of another friend's son," my guest said. "They found a doctor who has really helped him." That simple statement came as a huge relief—I was not alone. A path had already been cleared and walked by another family. This was the beginning of a networking process that eventually put us in touch with parents and families in all walks of life, fighting similar battles and having similar concerns. The Association for Retarded Citizens (ARC) along with Special Olympics provided a structure of activities for developmentally delayed citizens, and at the same time, offered supporting activities for the rest of the family. The ARC seeks to help people work through this series of questions:

- Why did this happen to my child?
- What can I do to help my child?
- What can I do to help all people with mental disabilities?

Our older children became involved in a Teens Aid the Retarded group and Michael, Karl's younger brother, benefited greatly from a class for younger siblings of mentally challenged people. The ARC is at the cutting edge of a movement striving for community-based opportunities and services for special needs people and their families. During the years we were actively involved, the organization began a half-way house and a self-advocate support group that functions with a complete set of officers and programs, selected and run by its members.

Acceptance and learning to live with the reality released us from unrealistic expectations and the stress and pressure that produced. Each of us is "deficient" in one way or another—compared to other people. One young friend of our daughter told her, "Everyone thinks that just because a person is mentally retarded, they can't be happy or sad, and that's just not true." We are not called to judge one another by artificial standards of IQ or appearance. We learned to let new acquaintances know, as soon as it was appropriate to do so that we had a family member who was mentally challenged. This saved people from embarrassing themselves with thoughtless comments about "retarded" people.

Understanding that "it is what it is" allowed us the freedom to celebrate Karl's progress and successes: learning to tie his shoes, to write his name, to control his bodily functions, to set the table correctly. We were no longer seeing each step as a small puzzle piece but rather as a piece enlarged and framed, a joyful end in its own right.

Appreciating the success of each day released us from the fear of tomorrow. The one day at a time approach gave us a sense of peace and serenity where tomorrow was truly another day.

Tomorrow may not be better or worse than today, but it will be different. And in that difference is the possibility of joy and pleasure. Life does go on.

I Don't Want to Lose You!

Three years and the pain is just as sharp
Confusing my faith, piercing my heart
Jabbing my consciousness

What is the point of it? Can there be a purpose?

I want to sleep in your bed, hold your teddy bear,
Stare into your deep blue eyes, hug your narrow shoulders.

The void is dark and deep, the pain endless.

My escapes work only for a while; then the truth rears and again,
At the source of my being, my face changes and my heart
pauses,
Awaiting the moment of reality.
Death is a silent heartbeat, and life as we know, is gone.

Is there no relief?

Time silently moves the clock, age creeps into my bones
The God I trusted is silent

Even as I try to embrace the pain
I still want to run and hide and start all over again.
I thought your specialness was a challenge
But no challenge rises to the level of this.

Susan Giesecke

I still cannot speak
Cannot utter words because
There are no words to express this void,
This pain, this no-thing

You lived bravely inspiring many,
A fine example of life and passion.
You made our lives richer, fuller, for knowing you.
You broadened our appreciation, our humbleness, our simplicity.
You made us better than we were.

I am weak from tears of remembering.
I don't want to lose you
And the sharpness of the pain says it.

—Susan Giesecke
October 24, 2013

100

Reflections from the Family

The purpose of this memoir is to share our family story and the specialness Karl brought to our lives. In addition, some have suggested this small book may be helpful to other families. So, here are some reflections and thoughts from his sister Laura and brother Michael.

I asked: "Would you share some of your personal thoughts regarding Karl and his life; his unique traits and what he may have taught you about life?"

Thoughts from LAURA LYNN:

I miss Karl. I love when he visits me in my dreams. And I enjoy watching *The Big Bang Theory* because there are so many behaviors and looks in the show that remind me of him. Whenever I shop, I always see something that I believe Karl would enjoy.

Karl being different was never a big deal. It just was what it was.

The general public has a view that mentally challenged people are all the same; eternally young, innocent, sweet and simple. We know differently. We know that the mentally challenged individual is an individual. Just like everyone else.

Karl displayed how IQ has no relation to common sense. Karl had common sense. He could problem solve. The solution may not have been socially appropriate, but he solved the problem!

IQ has no relation to appreciation of the arts and activities. Karl was unique. And I loved how he could appreciate WWF wrestling one night and have an equal appreciation for the opera the next day.

IQ has no relationship to maturing. Karl was a grown man who was allowed to show his love for toys, as many men do. Most assumed Karl would stay a child but he developed mature tastes. A surprising change was Happy Meals...he wanted the toy, but he didn't enjoy the meal. He amazed us when he asked for a salad. I never knew he would want a salad!

And Karl appreciated good-looking women. He was an adult male.

I admired Karl's creative ability. He displayed a great understanding of perception. His cardboard creations are awesome! And he was industrious, and always doing something.

I will always remember Karl's young years. As I look back, I cherish these memories: How Dad would rig things so they could not get broken (i.e. Attaching the Christmas Tree to the ceiling); Having to lie in bed with Karl, and many toys, to get him to stay in bed and go to sleep. And, of course, trying to sneak out when he had fallen asleep or falling asleep myself.

Karl grew into a wonderful adult. When we volunteered at the nursing home, he often did not want to go. But he went, and we would do little tasks like pouring ceramic molds.

I enjoyed when Karl would come and stay at the house with us. He would go to our events and hang at the house. BUT he always wanted to go home, and he would tell me every morning how many days were left until "Noel and Suz" would be back.

My greatest admiration for Karl developed watching him deal with his illness and hospital stay. He dealt with every situation! He just did what he had to do. He didn't try to eat when they told him he couldn't. He was brave.

One day I had to get on Karl because he wanted to watch TV and not go to physical therapy. I had to forcefully explain that he had to work in their schedule, not the other way around. And that he was my younger brother and he would need to be pushing his older sister in a wheelchair—not the other way around. Karl thought about it and went to rehab! Months later, I took Karl out of the facility for an outing. As we were walking out of a store, Karl told me that he was happy he could walk again. I was so PROUD of him! He had worked hard!

I have been blessed to have Karl as a brother. I miss him and will never be ready to say "Goodbye."

Love in a Teardrop

All day long the tear drops slip out
Dripping down my face.
No where to go,
No place to hide,
No going back.
So, it's come to this,
Love in a tear drop!

—Susan
Giesecke
October 24,
2013

Thoughts from MICHAEL:

Karl lived a simplistic life. He was happy doing arts and crafts, playing instruments, eating Happy Meals and watching movies. One thing I thought was very interesting about Karl was that he actually lived somewhat of a regimented life. If you didn't know better, you would think Karl was just watching TV all day. In reality, Karl had broken his day down by working on his inventions, playing instruments, playing his WII, shooting his Nerf guns, etc. Every day he would place his cardboard cutouts of his various women, his pictures and other important things around in perfect order.

Here is a funny story that I have told often. Karl had his Princess Leia cardboard cutout standing in her usual spot in front of the television. As I walked by, I grabbed the cutout like I was holding her in my arms, tilted it down like I was sweeping her off of her feet and giving her a kiss on the lips. Karl was absolutely livid that I would do such a thing to his lady. I had definitely crossed the line with that stunt!

Karl had a great imagination and he loved putting his imagination to use, turning his imagination into reality. That was a very important part of his life. If fact, if you put five cardboard tubes that were once used for wrapping paper and five gold bars in front of Karl and asked which one he wanted, he would undoubtedly choose the cardboard tubes. His needs were simple, and he lived in a world within his imagination. Almost like *Alice in Wonderland*. That is something that I could envy. If he wanted something, he would just create it! After Karl passed, we all marveled at his inventions we discovered—inventions we never even knew existed. Some of them were complicated and we had to study them as if we had stumbled upon an ancient Archimedes invention. He had an unbelievable memory on him as well. He could recall things that happened many years ago.

Karl was a loving person. He loved to give hugs and knew so many people. We could be out to dinner and people would stop by to say "Hello" to Karl.

Something else I found very interesting was Karl's ability to teach himself to play an instrument and even songs. He could literally play 20 plus instruments and he never had a single lesson on many of them. I remember him rewinding to a point in a movie or song on a tape recorder and teaching himself that song on an instrument, specifically the recorder. He would go through each key until he found the right one. He would go through it over and over again until he had the song mastered. He didn't write any of this down. He learned by listening, trying and memorizing. It was truly amazing. He also experienced great joy playing happy birthday on one of his instruments for birthdays. It was something simple that meant so much on your birthday!

Karl was also a person of strong conviction. There have been so many good and funny stories of Karl challenging the status quo. My favorite is a story from my wedding. Karl was *going* to be the best man at my wedding, and once he made up his mind, there was *no* changing it. Something else that I always thought was funny was our Thursday night dinners out. Whenever we went to Luby's, Karl loved to pick out extra food for the next day. He started out with one item, but eventually it grew into an entire meal and he used my tray to collect all his favorites. It was classic and there was no stopping him.

I remember all the times we would return from Colorado and it was time to unload the car. Dad, in vain, would do anything and everything in his powers to get Karl to help unload the van and no matter what, Karl just did not want to do this. We even tried just leaving Karl's stuff in the vehicle and when Karl needed something that was still in the car, he would just go and get that one item, leaving the rest of the stuff in the car. After ten plus years of fighting that losing battle, everybody just gave up trying to get Karl to help unload after trips. Maybe in a previous life he was a master negotiator!

From time to time, I would watch Karl while our parents were on vacation. No matter what, Karl was the boss! I would ask Karl what he wanted for dinner and he would ignore me. After multiple times, I was still ignored. Other times I would need to take him somewhere and he needed to put on his shoes, but he would take his time putting them on. Even though I was the one watching him, he always let me know that he was the boss.

I remember Karl going through his soft drink phase. At the end of the day he would have five or more empty Coke and Dr. Pepper cans sitting on the counter by his sofa. Sodas would disappear like water in the desert. I remember when Dad would come in from working outside looking to get a soft drink and they were all gone. So, we resorted to hiding the soft drinks under the bed or in the closet. Then, we would sneak around when we wanted a soft drink during the day. Karl would catch me with a can of Dr. Pepper from time to time and ask, "Where did you get that?" and then catching on that sodas were somewhere in the house. Of course, he found them. Eventually it got to the point where he didn't even want soft drinks anymore.

Karl was always a kid at heart. He loved his Happy Meals and the toys that came with them. I don't know how many times we would go to McDonalds trying to get ALL of the toys in that particular series. Those toys, to him, equated to some collector's Fabergé eggs. I remember looking through his clothes drawer and finding hardly any clothes but piles and piles of McDonald toys. To be honest, I loved going into his rooms and playing with his toys. He had a small arsenal of Nerf guns, toy swords and electronic gadgets. He was always a kid at heart and everybody, at some point in their life, had to envy him.

So, Karl taught me many different things. He taught me to march to the beat of my own drummer, to have conviction in the things I support, to live simply, and to collect the things that matter most.

Final Thoughts…

Ten years have passed so quickly—an eternity in a blink of an eye. There have been so many changes, yet some things never change. We have two new baby girls in the family, one named Chloe Leigh in honor of Karl. They are precious, full of life with wonderful smiles and twinkling eyes. We've explored the world, traveling in South America, the Baltic, and across the Atlantic to Spain. We carry on and on and on…

We are deeply grateful for our many blessings of family and friends.

When I look at young people, I marvel at their wholesome good looks, their energy and enthusiasm for life. I want to help them make the most of each day, so unique and so special. I want to build a protective bubble over them.

My attitude toward time has changed. I'm willing now to remain quiet, observing nature and experiencing the joy of being. I treasure each day and the opportunity it brings for work and service and play.

Music has become my religion, my contact with the ephemeral. The abstractness of music encompasses my life now. There are no limitations of speech or page.

I understand pain too. Recently, within days I met two lost parents, missing their children. One, a woman, said, "Part of my heart is gone, and I can't get over it." I replied, "And you don't want to 'get over it,' do you?" She agreed. The other, a man my age, a stranger, held my hand during a musical performance, and we both cried.

A cousin shared recently that Aunt Peg, who lost her daughter twelve years ago, *soldiers on*, but she's not the same. Yes, those words are apt; *soldiering on*, yet not the same. All trauma produces such a change, I'm sure. The loss of a loved child includes a loss of identity, a loss of routine, and a loss of the future.

I no longer wear mascara because I don't know when or what will make me cry. My wardrobe is predominantly black. I no longer think long range. One day at a time is sufficient. Now is good.

I have no patience for people who complain or judge others. Life is too short, too precious. My empathy for those who suffer and those who lose loved ones through tragedy and war knows no bounds. I can no longer watch violence on television. The Biblical psalms lamenting the trials of life, are my daily meditations.

So many platitudes, such as "He's in a better place," "he's not suffering anymore," "he's whole now," "he's an angel with God," "you'll be together again," "you don't have to worry about outliving Karl now," are meaningless, almost cruel.

All my concepts of God and eternity have left me weak and childlike. Did I ever "believe"? What is worthy of worship? What if I can't reconcile life experience with a belief system? Do I even *need* a belief system? Like a child, I am open to being led and directed, open to question and explore. Life suddenly has no boundaries; the picture frame has no border. It's a floating nebulous cloud. I even question long-standing relationships that feel fuzzy and distant.

When everything crumbles and you fear exploding at any minute, what holds you together? Time and encouragement from friends who have walked the path: "It will get better," they assure. Beauty and function: When I read history of the arts and sciences, I realize, in spite of much pain and suffering, the immense progress mankind has made. I marvel in gratitude and humility.

Yes, life does go on, as it must. Each of us is an altered soul, unique in our own histories and personalities—wounded, with healed-over scars, soldiering on.

Karl's scholarship is fully-funded now, and we've had the pleasure of meeting several recipients in person. Karl will be missed, but not forgotten. Life does continue in the lives of those we support and inspire. And the broader the circle we can create, the better.

I love teaching ESL and sharing financial planning strategies through volunteering. Mentoring a student through their formative years is truly rewarding. Nurturing a plant and young fish brings pure joy.

And, the greatest learning of all: learning to accept. Karl's life was a gift we did not expect. Only when we accepted his uniqueness did he blossom. When we accepted him as he was, we grew too. The gifts he left us have been unexpected too. And we still struggle with the fear that by accepting his loss, he will be truly gone.

And in that fear is a gift too. Karl was truly loved and will not be forgotten.

Susan Giesecke

"nsgiesecke@sbcglobal.net"

Karl

You are forever a part of me
When I see a boat
A colorful cart model
You are here!

When I sit down to eat
And see a shrimp cocktail
On the menu or on the table
You are here!

When the captain calls
Or an officer passes
I see you saluting
You are here!

Happy sailing dear one!

—Susan Giesecke
June 14, 2015

112

Graduation

CPSIA information can be obtained
at www.ICGtesting.com
Printed in the USA
LVHW020256300121
677616LV00006B/724

9 781647 191160